# World Religions Workbook

Christopher D. Rodkey

ICONOCLASTIC PRESS
Denville, New Jersey

Printed and distributed by Lulu.

*An Instructor's Edition is also available.*

Rodkey, Christopher D. (1977-  )
    World Religions Workbook.  Student Edition.
ISBN  978-1-4116-9621-1  (pbk.)

    I. World Religions. II. World Religions (Textbooks). III. Religious
Education (Secondary Textbooks). IV.  Religious Education
(Confirmation Textbooks). V.  Philosophical Education (Adolescent). VI.
Author. VII.  Title.

# Table of Contents

# Preface

This workbook is designed for an introductory course in world or comparative religions for high school, college, seminary students, or Confirmation/Coming of Age students. It is designed to be a helpful resource for you to use in your class that you can later put it on your bookshelf and use as a reference text after your class is over. The motivation for such a book arises from my beliefs that the basic study of world religions is salient for a balanced liberal arts education, and that the knowledge gained from such a course has relevance outside of the classroom: in the study of other disciplines, in the world of business, and in the daily life of good citizenship and being a good neighbor.

The worksheets are to be filled out by you with the guidance or direction of your class instructor. This book can be used as a supplement to a traditional world religions textbook or it can be used alone in a classroom. The workbook contains a glossary of terms used in my own classrooms (for high school, college, and graduate/professional students) to help you in your research on a variety of academic levels.

Note that the glossary terminology includes several philosophical and theological terms, as this book can be used to aid in philosophical education, particularly at the high school or college level. It is my conviction that philosophical reasoning—as well as theological self-reflection—is an essential element in the introductory study of world religions. In other words, I believe that after one learns about the world religions, one should consider *what it means* that there is more than one claim to "truth" in the world, and how "I" approach these various claims to truth. Some of the questions that I hope are provoked include: What are my own belief(s) about these claims to truth? How are they validated? Do I even need to validate them? How might my beliefs contribute (or detract) from good citizenship or being a good neighbor? At the end, it is my hope for my students and readers that despite whatever your religious beliefs are (which includes atheistic or non-theistic beliefs), that you might articulate them well and learn to speak responsibly and humbly to others who are religiously different than you.

\* \* \*

This workbook was actually suggested to me by my college students, who struggled with photocopies of these pages and recognized that my worksheets have a value beyond being study guides. For their feedback, I thank my students; and I hope that this demonstrates to them that they are an essential part of the academic work of their professors, something they might not hear enough. I also wish to acknowledge my confirmation class students, who are naturally interested in world religions and are an inspiration to me that the younger generations will be more tolerant than my and my elders' generations.

I thank the Community Church of Mountain Lakes, United Church of Christ, for allowing me flexibility with my schedule to work on this book. I also

2

wish to acknowledge the pastoral staff of the church for pastoral and professional support in my role as pastor-teacher in our church and the community.

As this is my first published book, I should also recognize all of my teachers, who instilled in my a love of learning, despite my resistance and contrariness as a student and learner. I cannot name them all here, for risk of omitting many names, but I would like to thank all of my teachers, from my earliest years through my doctoral education, especially those who interested me in the philosophy of religion and the study of world religions.

To the religious educators, youth ministers, clergy of all faiths who work with teenagers, high school religion teachers, and especially volunteers who teach confirmation classes: your work is essential to the continuance of our human race and faithful societies. I thank you all for your hard work and I can only hope that this book might aid you in it.

To my parents; my grandparents; and in particular, my spouse, Traci, who all have always supported my intellectual pursuits, I offer a great debt of gratitude. Traci, to whom this book is dedicated, has supported this project from the beginning and is always my core support. This book exists as a testament to her patience and generosity.

Christopher D. Rodkey
April, 2006

# World Religion Worksheets

# Worksheet for
# Native American Religions

Other Name(s) of Religion:

Year and Location Founded:

Where Located Today:

Major Figure(s) and Significance:

Primary Beliefs:

Major Sects, Branches, or Denominations:

Major Historical Events:

Holy Text(s) and Use:

Belief(s) about God(s):

Belief about Humans (Theological Anthropology):

Belief about Women and/or Sexuality:

Belief about Creation:

Belief about the End (Eschatology):

Belief about History (Historiography):

Other beliefs about Reality (Metaphysics):

Belief about art (Aesthetics):

Famous Constituents:

**Notes**

# Worksheet for
# African Religions

Other Name(s) of Religion:

Year and Location Founded:

Where Located Today:

Major Figure(s) and Significance:

Primary Beliefs:

Major Sects, Branches, or Denominations:

Major Historical Events:

Holy Text(s) and Use:

Belief(s) about God(s):

Belief about Humans (Theological Anthropology):

Belief about Women and/or Sexuality:

Belief about Creation:

Belief about the End (Eschatology):

Belief about History (Historiography):

Other beliefs about Reality (Metaphysics):

Belief about art (Aesthetics):

Famous Constituents:

**Notes**

# Worksheet for
# Hinduism

Other Name(s) of Religion:

Year and Location Founded:

Where Located Today:

Major Figure(s) and Significance:

Primary Beliefs:

Major Sects, Branches, or Denominations:

Major Historical Events:

Holy Text(s) and Use:

Belief(s) about God(s):

Belief about Humans (Theological Anthropology):

Belief about Women and/or Sexuality:

Belief about Creation:

Belief about the End (Eschatology):

Belief about History (Historiography):

Other beliefs about Reality (Metaphysics):

Belief about art (Aesthetics):

Famous Constituents:

**Notes**

# Worksheet for
# Buddhism

Other Name(s) of Religion:

Year and Location Founded:

Where Located Today:

Major Figure(s) and Significance:

Primary Beliefs:

Major Sects, Branches, or Denominations:

Major Historical Events:

Holy Text(s) and Use:

Belief(s) about God(s):

Belief about Humans (Theological Anthropology):

Belief about Women and/or Sexuality:

Belief about Creation:

Belief about the End (Eschatology):

Belief about History (Historiography):

Other beliefs about Reality (Metaphysics):

Belief about art (Aesthetics):

Famous Constituents:

**Notes**

# Worksheet for
# Jainism

Other Name(s) of Religion:

Year and Location Founded:

Where Located Today:

Major Figure(s) and Significance:

Primary Beliefs:

Major Sects, Branches, or Denominations:

Major Historical Events:

Holy Text(s) and Use:

Belief(s) about God(s):

Belief about Humans (Theological Anthropology):

Belief about Women and/or Sexuality:

Belief about Creation:

Belief about the End (Eschatology):

Belief about History (Historiography):

Other beliefs about Reality (Metaphysics):

Belief about art (Aesthetics):

Famous Constituents:

**Notes**

# Worksheet for
# Sikhism

Other Name(s) of Religion:

Year and Location Founded:

Where Located Today:

Major Figure(s) and Significance:

Primary Beliefs:

Major Sects, Branches, or Denominations:

Major Historical Events:

Holy Text(s) and Use:

Belief(s) about God(s):

Belief about Humans (Theological Anthropology):

Belief about Women and/or Sexuality:

Belief about Creation:

Belief about the End (Eschatology):

Belief about History (Historiography):

Other beliefs about Reality (Metaphysics):

Belief about art (Aesthetics):

Famous Constituents:

**Notes**

# Worksheet for Confucianism

Other Name(s) of Religion:

Year and Location Founded:

Where Located Today:

Major Figure(s) and Significance:

Primary Beliefs:

Major Sects, Branches, or Denominations:

Major Historical Events:

Holy Text(s) and Use:

Belief(s) about God(s):

Belief about Humans (Theological Anthropology):

Belief about Women and/or Sexuality:

Belief about Creation:

Belief about the End (Eschatology):

Belief about History (Historiography):

Other beliefs about Reality (Metaphysics):

Belief about art (Aesthetics):

Famous Constituents:

**Notes**

# Worksheet for
# Taoism

Other Name(s) of Religion:

Year and Location Founded:

Where Located Today:

Major Figure(s) and Significance:

Primary Beliefs:

Major Sects, Branches, or Denominations:

Major Historical Events:

Holy Text(s) and Use:

Belief(s) about God(s):

Belief about Humans (Theological Anthropology):

Belief about Women and/or Sexuality:

Belief about Creation:

Belief about the End (Eschatology):

Belief about History (Historiography):

Other beliefs about Reality (Metaphysics):

Belief about art (Aesthetics):

Famous Constituents:

**Notes**

# Worksheet for
# Shinto

Other Name(s) of Religion:

Year and Location Founded:

Where Located Today:

Major Figure(s) and Significance:

Primary Beliefs:

Major Sects, Branches, or Denominations:

Major Historical Events:

Holy Text(s) and Use:

Belief(s) about God(s):

Belief about Humans (Theological Anthropology):

Belief about Women and/or Sexuality:

Belief about Creation:

Belief about the End (Eschatology):

Belief about History (Historiography):

Other beliefs about Reality (Metaphysics):

Belief about art (Aesthetics):

Famous Constituents:

**Notes**

# Worksheet for
# Zoroastrianism

Other Name(s) of Religion:

Year and Location Founded:

Where Located Today:

Major Figure(s) and Significance:

Primary Beliefs:

Major Sects, Branches, or Denominations:

Major Historical Events:

Holy Text(s) and Use:

Belief(s) about God(s):

Belief about Humans (Theological Anthropology):

Belief about Women and/or Sexuality:

Belief about Creation:

Belief about the End (Eschatology):

Belief about History (Historiography):

Other beliefs about Reality (Metaphysics):

Belief about art (Aesthetics):

Famous Constituents:

**Notes**

# Worksheet for
# Judaism

Other Name(s) of Religion:

Year and Location Founded:

Where Located Today:

Major Figure(s) and Significance:

Primary Beliefs:

Major Sects, Branches, or Denominations:

Major Historical Events:

Holy Text(s) and Use:

Belief(s) about God(s):

Belief about Humans (Theological Anthropology):

Belief about Women and/or Sexuality:

Belief about Creation:

Belief about the End (Eschatology):

Belief about History (Historiography):

Other beliefs about Reality (Metaphysics):

Belief about art (Aesthetics):

Famous Constituents:

**Notes**

# Worksheet for Christianity

Other Name(s) of Religion:

Year and Location Founded:

Where Located Today:

Major Figure(s) and Significance:

Primary Beliefs:

Major Sects, Branches, or Denominations:

Major Historical Events:

Holy Text(s) and Use:

Belief(s) about God(s):

Belief about Humans (Theological Anthropology):

Belief about Women and/or Sexuality:

Belief about Creation:

Belief about the End (Eschatology):

Belief about History (Historiography):

Other beliefs about Reality (Metaphysics):

Belief about art (Aesthetics):

Famous Constituents:

**Notes**

# Worksheet for
# Islam

Other Name(s) of Religion:

Year and Location Founded:

Where Located Today:

Major Figure(s) and Significance:

Primary Beliefs:

Major Sects, Branches, or Denominations:

Major Historical Events:

Holy Text(s) and Use:

Belief(s) about God(s):

Belief about Humans (Theological Anthropology):

Belief about Women and/or Sexuality:

Belief about Creation:

Belief about the End (Eschatology):

Belief about History (Historiography):

Other beliefs about Reality (Metaphysics):

Belief about art (Aesthetics):

Famous Constituents:

**Notes**

# Worksheet for
# The Baha'i Faith

Other Name(s) of Religion:

Year and Location Founded:

Where Located Today:

Major Figure(s) and Significance:

Primary Beliefs:

Major Sects, Branches, or Denominations:

Major Historical Events:

Holy Text(s) and Use:

Belief(s) about God(s):

Belief about Humans (Theological Anthropology):

Belief about Women and/or Sexuality:


Belief about Creation:


Belief about the End (Eschatology):


Belief about History (Historiography):


Other beliefs about Reality (Metaphysics):


Belief about art (Aesthetics):


Famous Constituents:

**Notes**

# Worksheet for
# Neo-Pagan Religions

Other Name(s) of Religion:

Year and Location Founded:

Where Located Today:

Major Figure(s) and Significance:

Primary Beliefs:

Major Sects, Branches, or Denominations:

Major Historical Events:

Holy Text(s) and Use:

Belief(s) about God(s):

Belief about Humans (Theological Anthropology):

Belief about Women and/or Sexuality:

Belief about Creation:

Belief about the End (Eschatology):

Belief about History (Historiography):

Other beliefs about Reality (Metaphysics):

Belief about art (Aesthetics):

Famous Constituents:

**Notes**

# Worksheet for
# Contemporary Atheisms

Other Name(s) of Religion:

Year and Location Founded:

Where Located Today:

Major Figure(s) and Significance:


Primary Beliefs:


Major Sects, Branches, or Denominations:


Major Historical Events:


Holy Text(s) and Use:


Belief(s) about God(s):


Belief about Humans (Theological Anthropology):

Belief about Women and/or Sexuality:

Belief about Creation:

Belief about the End (Eschatology):

Belief about History (Historiography):

Other beliefs about Reality (Metaphysics):

Belief about art (Aesthetics):

Famous Constituents:

**Notes**

# Worksheet for
# Other Religions #1

Other Name(s) of Religion:

Year and Location Founded:

Where Located Today:

Major Figure(s) and Significance:

Primary Beliefs:

Major Sects, Branches, or Denominations:

Major Historical Events:

Holy Text(s) and Use:

Belief(s) about God(s):

Belief about Humans (Theological Anthropology):

Belief about Women and/or Sexuality:

Belief about Creation:

Belief about the End (Eschatology):

Belief about History (Historiography):

Other beliefs about Reality (Metaphysics):

Belief about art (Aesthetics):

Famous Constituents:

**Notes**

# Worksheet for
# Other Religions #2

Other Name(s) of Religion:

Year and Location Founded:

Where Located Today:

Major Figure(s) and Significance:

Primary Beliefs:

Major Sects, Branches, or Denominations:

Major Historical Events:

Holy Text(s) and Use:

Belief(s) about God(s):

Belief about Humans (Theological Anthropology):

Belief about Women and/or Sexuality:

Belief about Creation:

Belief about the End (Eschatology):

Belief about History (Historiography):

Other beliefs about Reality (Metaphysics):

Belief about art (Aesthetics):

Famous Constituents:

**Notes**

# Glossary of Helpful Terms

**Aesthetics** • Philosophical discipline which considers beauty; often called the "philosophy of art."

**Alterity** • Term to describe "otherness" by one person or group to another.

**Animism** • Meaning "the doctrine of spiritual beings," coined by E. B. Tylor (1832-1917 CE), *animism* usually refers to the religious belief "in," or placing religious significance to specific aspects of nature or living things. *See Paganism, Pantheism, Panentheism.*

**Anonymous Christian** • Term used by some Christians to describe their belief about other religions, that other "legitimate" religions, when practiced properly, are really Christians, but do not yet realize their own Christianity. *See K. Rahner, Inclusivism.*

**Apocalypticism** • In Western religions, especially Christianity, the consideration of "hidden things" or a "revealing" of ultimate knowledge. *See Eschatology.*

**Aquinas, St. Thomas** • Catholic Christian philosopher, theologian and saint (c. 1225-1274 CE) who formulated the *teleological* and *cosmological arguments* for the existence of God. *See Teleological Argument, Cosmological Argument.*

**Atheism** • The rejection of belief in a god or gods, or the specific rejection of *classical theism*. As such, following the latter definition, the term "atheism" is sometimes used by those with a traditionally *classically-theistic* religion (usually Christians or Muslims) to describe those whose religions are not deemed legitimate or correct. *See Classical Theism, Theism, Non-Theism.*

**Augustine, Saint** • Important philosopher and theologian (354-430 CE) who wrote about how Christians should view those who are not Christian and on the value of non-Christian arts and letters. Conversely, St. Augustine also made a clear distinction between *pagans* and *heretics*: *pagans* are those of religions other than Christianity or Judaism and *heretics* have categorically rejected Christianity. *See Pagan, Heretics.*

**Barth, Karl** • Contemporary theologian (1886-1968 CE) who argued in his *Church Dogmatics* that Christians must be tolerant of other religions as "idolaters," as Christians should be tolerant of Christians also as "idolaters" themselves. Barth was also a Universalist, believing that no one will be damned. *See Universalism.*

**BCE** · *See Before the Common Era.*

**Before the Common Era** · Abbreviated "BCE," Common Era is a controversial (though generally accepted by academics) politically-correct re-labeling of Before Christ, or *AD*. *See Common Era.*

**Biblical Literalism** · A Christian form of *literalism*, where a reader of the Bible does not acknowledge interpretive distance between herself and the text. *See Literalism, Biblical Theology, Hermeneutics, Fundamentalism.*

**Biblical Theology** · Usually a Jewish or Christian sub-discipline of Biblical studies or theology which is interested in the consistency or adhering principles between the varying books of the Hebrew Bible and the New Testament. *See Hermeneutics.*

**CE** · *See Common Era.*

**Classical Theism** · The belief in a strictly transcendent God (that is, God is outside of space and time), where God is clearly separated from 'His' creation. At one time, c*lassical theism* was called t*heism*; some *atheisms* are a specific rejection of *classical* theism. *See Theism, Atheism.*

**Common Era** · Abbreviated "CE," Common Era is a controversial (though generally accepted by academics) politically-correct re-labeling of *anno Domini*, or *AD*. *See Before the Common Era.*

**Cosmological Argument** · An argument for the existence of God, associated with *St. Thomas Aquinas*, that God is the first cause or "mover" in the universe. *See T. Aquinas, Teleological Argument, Ontological Argument.*

**Cosmology** · In philosophy, the study of the universe as a whole and in particular, the location of humans in the larger scheme of the universe.

**Cult** · In religious studies, *cult* can have two meanings. First, *cult* may simply refer to a group of religious practices in any religion. Second, *cult* often refers to a religious group considered to be outside of the "mainstream" of the dominant society; the use of this term is usually pejorative. *See Sect, Denomination, Occult.*

**Deep Pantheism** · A modification of *pantheism*, construed as a rejection of *panentheism*, which attempts to avoid placing a limitation on conceptions of "nature," so as to posit a nearly-infinite *cosmological* understanding of "nature." This term was coined by the American philosophical theologian Robert Corrington. *See Pantheism, Panentheism.*

**Denomination** · Term usually used in Hinduism and Christianity which refers to the major, well-established "branches" or "sub-groups" which constitute the majority of adherents. See *Sect, Cult.*

**Deism** · The belief, associated closely with *classical theism*, that God created and designed the world, and has since left creation. See *Classical Theism, Transcendence.*

**Dualism** · When speaking about God, *dualism* usually means the belief in two gods or two forces which guide or rule over reality. These two forces or gods are usually opposites or enemies of each other. *See Monotheism, Polytheism.*

**Differential Pluralism** · The philosophical belief that all cultures and all religions naturally "fit together." *Differential pluralism* is a position that arises from Christian process theology, and was coined by the theologian Catharine Keller. *See Pluralism, Identist pluralism, Synchronism.*

**Eschatology** · Primarily in Western religions, the theological consideration of the end of the world or the "last days." *See Apocalypticism.*

**Exclusivism** · A position where an individual believes that only one or one's group (broadly defined) is the true religion. *See Inclusivism.*

**Fundamentalism** · An *exclusivistic* or *ideologically totalized* position, usually associated with one of the large "world religions," which requires adherents (and possibly all of those around the adherents) to strictly believe in a singular interpretation of the religion or the religion's scripture. Fundamentalists may be part of a specific sect or a movement within established religious groups. Although fundamentalists usually have a very direct theology, usually a fundamentalist does not acknowledge any interpretation of a religion or religious text and claims to have "pure" knowledge from a God or Gods, or the spiritual meaning of religious texts. Sometimes fundamentalism is associated with terrorism. The term *fundamentalism* was initially a Christian word that meant a specific "return" to Christian "fundamentals," that is, certain specific theological beliefs. *See Exclusivism, Ideological Totalism.*

**Ghose, Sri Aurobindo** · Indian Hindu activist and philosopher (1872-1950 CE) who argued for a new "catholicity" of Hinduism, that opposite religious claims could be tolerated within a singular, pluralistic religious system.

**Henotheism** · A *polytheistic* religious system (that is, having many gods), where one god or godly principle is the leading or dominant god over other gods. *See Polytheism.*

**Heresy** · A belief that is considered to be a direct rejection of what is considered an orthodox belief, usually in Western religions. *See Heretic, Heterodoxy, Fundamentalism.*

**Heretic** · One who believes in *heresies. See Heresy, Heterodoxy, Augustine.*

**Hermeneutics** · In philosophy, the consideration of interpretation: interpretation of texts, art, or reality itself. *See Literalism, Biblical Theology.*

**Heterodoxy** · Within a larger religious scheme, beliefs which transgress against either the dominant or "orthodox" beliefs. *See Orthodoxy, Heresy.*

**Hick, John** · British philosopher (1922- ) who wrote that *exclusivism* is incompatible with a Christian theology, and instead advocated for a Christian *pluralistic* theology that is also *universalist. See Pluralism, Universalism.*

**Historiography** · In theology, an understanding of the nature of history, its various epochs, and also how a religious consideration of time might influence a culture's understanding of history.

**Identitist Pluralism** · A philosophical position which acknowledges the *pluralism*, or diversity, of different religions; believes that all religions are the same; and that the differences between religions is primarily a matter of difference in language. The Baha'i Faith is in some ways a *identitist pluralism.* See *Pluralism, Differential Pluralism.*

**Ideological Totalism** · In religion, a theological or philosophical position which requires adherents of a group to have an absolute or total submission of belief to a teaching, leader, or organization. *See Cult, Fundamentalism.*

**Immanence** · An understanding of divinity being present in the world. *See Deism, Transcendence.*

**Inclusivism** · A position where one believes that one's own religion is the true religion, but others *may be* true. *See Exclusivism, Pluralism.*

**Literalism** · An interpretive or *hermeneutic* position which interprets a religious or sacred text literally, without acknowledging any interpretive distance between the reader and the text. *See Biblical Literalism, Biblical Theology, Fundamentalism, Hermeneutics.*

**Kung, Hans** · Catholic Christian theologian (1928- ) whose philosophical position drew a strong line between what is individual, local faith and the more universal, public notion of plurality or religions.

**Metaphysics** · In philosophy, a very general term which refers to a philosophical consideration of the whole of reality, as opposed to the physical sciences; the term literally means "after physics." In *occultism*, the term means a religious consideration of reality, as a kind of theology outside of mainstream religions or Christianity. *See Cosmology, Ontology, Philosophy of Religion.*

**New Age Religion** · A broad term that refers to a religious practice that is highly individual and is often integrative of numerous varying mainstream and *occult* religious practices. The term also refers to new religious movements which sometimes defy definition or categorization within the schema of mainstream religions. New Age religions might be best exemplified by the then-fictional "Church of All Worlds" described in Robert Heinlein's (1907-1988 CE) 1961 novel, *Stranger in a Strange Land.* See *Cult, Occult, Pagan.*

**Nicholas of Cusa** · A theologian (1404-1464 CE) who wrote the first non-polemic Christian engagement of Islam, *De Pace Fidei* (*On Peaceful Unity of Faith*). He later wrote an important polemic text where he argued that the Qur'an can be a religiously good text, but only with a Christian interpretation.

**Non-Theism** · A religious system that either has no belief in god or gods, or a religion for which the belief in divinity is not important or irrelevant in the larger scheme of the religious system. *See Atheism.*

**Occult** · Broad term, literally meaning "secret," which explores religious topics outside of the religious mainstream in the West (which many so-called *cults* would also reject) such as magic, dream interpretation, astral-body projection, numerology, extra-sensory perception, and extraterrestrial lore. Sometimes *occult* practices can be described as a poaching of pagan or tribal religious customs. *See Cult, New Age Religion, Paganism.*

**Ontological Argument** · Argument for the existence of God proposed by St. Anselm of Canterbury (1033/1034-11-9 CE) that if humans can conceive of a greatest conceivable being, then such a being must be real both in the real world as well as in the mind. *See Teleological Argument, Cosmological Argument.*

**Ontology** · Philosophical sub-discipline of *metaphysics* which considers being itself or foundational existence, and the varying categories of being. *See Metaphysics, Philosophy of Religion.*

**Orthodoxy** · Literally meaning "right teaching" or "right worship," *orthodoxy* usually refers to the generally-accepted religious beliefs or doctrines of a particular religious group, though it often refers to the dominant beliefs of a religious group—despite whether the beliefs are actually doctrinally held by the dominant group. Furthermore, it should be noted that *orthodoxies* usually arise for political or social reasons, and not simply for theological or doctrinal reasons; as such "orthodoxies" are constructed. *See Heterodoxy, Fundamentalism.*

**Pagan** ▪ Broad term with several meanings. First, *pagan* literally means "country dweller," and suggests someone who is religiously outside of the mainstream and may have tribal or animistic religious beliefs. Second, the term can refer to a theological position that attaches divinity to land or space. Third, in a pejorative sense, in Christianity and Islam, *pagan* refers to someone who is not of the mainstream religion but does not necessarily have knowledge of the "true religion"; that is, the *pagan* is not someone who rejects the true religion, he or she simply has no knowledge of the true religion. Fourth, *pagan* sometimes refers to the tribal religions of the European continent. Fifth, in contemporary usage, in Christianity or Islam, *pagan* again can mean someone outside of the mainstream religion; or a *pagan* is a self-descriptive word for a person whose religion is not mainstream, nor necessarily part of a *cult*, *New Age*, or *occult* group. Rather, the person integrates into one's religious practices elements of ancient or tribal religions which are typically nature-based. Sixth, *pagan* can refer to a person who integrates any feminine aspect of divinity or Goddess-worship into one's religious practices; often this use of *pagan* is called "neo-pagan." *See Animism, Pantheism, Panentheism, New Age Religion, Augustine.*

**Pantheism** ▪ A religious belief that god is *immanent*, that is, completely present in the world or universe. In *pantheism* there is no *transcendence*, which is to say, there is not an understanding of God being outside or unconditioned by space and time. For many *classical theists,* pantheism may be thought of as the opposite of classical theism, and, as such, pantheistic religions are sometimes described by classical theists as *atheistic. See Immanence, Transcendence, Panentheism, Deep Pantheism.*

**Panentheism** ▪ A combination of *pantheism* and *classical theism*, a religious belief that God is both *transcendent* and *immanent*. In other words, God is present wholly in the world or universe (having immanence), *and* God is also outside of space and time (transcendence). Sometimes called "the God of the Philosophers," *panentheism* is attributed to the 19<sup>th</sup> century philosophers *F. Schleiermacher* and F. Schlegel, and the 20<sup>th</sup> century theologians *P. Tillich*, J. Cobb, and D. Tracy. *See Transcendence, Immanence, P. Tillich, F. Schleiermacher, Deep Pantheism.*

**Philosophical Anthropology** ▪ A theological consideration of human existence and nature, as well as human meaning. *See Theological Anthropology.*

**Philosophy** ▪ Literally, "the love of wisdom"; more generally, a reasoned approached to the "big questions." *See Theology.*

**Philosophy of Religion** ▪ Philosophical sub-discipline of metaphysics which considers, validates, and scrutinizes the claims that religions make. *See Metaphysics, Ontology.*

**Pluralism** · Philosophical position which acknowledges religious diversity. *See Differential Pluralism, Identitist Pluralism, Inclusivism, Exclusivism, Synchronism.*

**Polytheism** · A belief in two or more gods. *See Dualism, Henotheism.*

**Ritual** · Any action, or set of actions, performed corporately or acknowledged corporately by a religion. A ritual may be said to "construct reality," which is to say, ritual has the ability to manipulate an individual or community's being in or perception of the world.

**Quasi-Religious** · A system of beliefs that may be religious or take on religious characteristics (ritual, holy texts, religious authority of leaders) but does not claim to be a religion. For theologian and philosopher Paul Tillich, quasi-religions are typically political ideologies (such as communism), patriotism, or nationalism—for Tillich, these are *quasi-religious* because they are not rooted in something "ultimate." *See P. Tillich.*

**Rahner, Karl** · A Catholic Christian theologian (1904-1984 CE) who believed that those of legitimate, non-Christian religions, who follow their religions properly, are really *anonymous Christians. See Anonymous Christian.*

**Religion** · A system of beliefs about the nature of reality (metaphysics), the nature of truth and knowledge (epistemology), and human meaning and existence (theological anthropology). Religious knowledge differs from other kinds of knowledge, as religious knowledge is explicitly based upon the *belief in beliefs*, as opposed to be the belief in facts.

**Schleiermacher, Friedrich** · German "Idealist" philosopher and theologian (1768-1834 CE) to whom the idea of *panentheism* is attributed. See *panentheism.*

**Sect** · In Islam, a sect is a major branch of the religion. Otherwise, a sect is a branch of a larger religious group, often with very specific ideological or theological differences with the larger group. *See Cult, Denomination.*

**Spinoza, Baruch** · Jewish philosopher (1632-1677 CE) who advocated for a *pantheistic* version of Judaism, and was later expelled from his religious community. Friedrich Schleiermacher called *pantheism* "Spinozism" in his book, *On Religion.* See *pantheism; F. Schleiermacher.*

**Tashakanron** · A philosophical methodology or position which acknowledges tensions between the individual's faith and the plurality of the community, so that religious dialogue is to be understood as a "discourse with many subjectivities" (or many people). *Tashakanron* is largely rooted in Chinese philosophy, but was coined by the philosopher Gereon Kopf. *See Pluralism, Differential Pluralism.*

**Synchronism** • In Egyptology or archaeology, *synchronism* is when records, texts, or artifacts' dates, information, or very existence are historically or theoretically consistent with each other. In theology, *synchronism* may be thought of as a kind of *pluralism*—that is, an acknowledgement that more than one religion exists in the larger system of the world at this time—or an integration of varying religious elements, usually from current mainstream religions—by an individual or religious community. *See Pluralism, Identitist Pluralism, Paganism.*

**Teleological Argument** • An argument for the existence of God, associated with *St. Thomas Aquinas*, that the universe is so full of design that some infinite being—that is, God—had to design it. *See Teleology, T. Aquinas.*

**Teleology** • Philosophical position that the universe is designed or purposed; typically associated with the ancient Greek philosopher, Aristotle (384-322 BCE). *See Teleological Argument, T. Aquinas.*

**Theism** • The belief in a god or gods. *See Classical Theism.*

**Theological Anthropology** • A theological consideration of human existence and nature, as well as human meaning. *See Philosophical Anthropology.*

**Theology** • Literally meaning "God-talk," *theology* is a reasoned consideration of religious topics, especially of the idea, nature, and meaning of "God." *See philosophy.*

**Tillich, Paul** • German-American philosopher and theologian (1886-1965 CE) who coined the category of the *quasi-religious* and posited all religious perspectives, even those which are contradictory, as philosophically posited similarly (though with varying degrees of validity) in response to "Being-Itself." *See Quasi-Religious, Panentheism.*

**Transcendence** • In theology, a term which usually refers to the remoteness, or *alterity*, of divinity, but can also refer to the divine's actual or ultimate involvement in reality as the foundation of being. *See Deism, Immanence, Panentheism, Classical Theism.*

**Unitarianism** • In Christianity, the rejection of a "Trinitarian," or three-part, divinity, in preference to a singular, unified divinity. *See Deism, Unitarian-Universalism.*

**Unitarian-Universalism** • In the 20th century, organized Unitarians and Universalists in the United States merged to create the *Unitarian-Universalist Association.* Today, Unitarian-Universalists do not consider themselves a Christian denomination, but rather, a separate movement. *See Unitarianism, Universalism.*

**Universalism** · The belief, usually in western religions, that there is no possibility of damnation or that there is no punishment in the afterlife. *See K. Barth, Unitarian-Universalism.*

## Other terms & notes

# Other terms & notes

# About the Author

**Christopher D. Rodkey**, originally from Columbia, Pennsylvania, has a B.A. (honors, philosophy and English) from Saint Vincent College, the M.Div. degree from the University of Chicago, and is a Ph.D. candidate in philosophical and theological studies at Drew University. He was also a Research Fellow for the Youth Theological Initiative, Candler School of Theology at Emory University, Atlanta, Georgia.

Rodkey, who is a Licensed Pastor in the New Jersey Association of the United Church of Christ, is Youth Pastor and Teacher at The Community Church of Mountain Lakes (United Church of Christ) in Mountain Lakes, New Jersey. He also teaches at Drew University, New Jersey City University, County College of Morris, and Bergen Community College. In addition, he privately consults corporations and non-profit organizations.

Rodkey has published in numerous journals in the areas of contemporary philosophy and theology, liturgics, music, and youth ministry.

He and his family live in northern New Jersey. He can be reached at cdrodkey@yahoo.com.

CPSIA information can be obtained
at www.ICGtesting.com
Printed in the USA
LVHW100236280819
629213LV00003B/36/P